Weird !

from Around

the World

Hundreds of

Bizarre Laws

MANIK JOSHI

<u>Dedication</u>

THIS

BOOK

IS

DEDICATED

TO

ALL

WEIRD

PEOPLE

IN

THE

WORLD!

Copyright Notice

DISCLAIMER

Most of the laws in this book have been verified. But many have been taken from sources which do not include law citations. I don't encourage the reader to execute any of these laws in court, without getting them verified by an attorney.

Table of Contents

01. Weird Laws -- Australia

01. It is against the law for children to purchase alcohol, cigarettes, but they are not prohibited from using them.

02. It is against the law to be drunk in a pub.

03. It is against the law to be near or inside a house that is used by thieves regularly. [Vagrancy Act of 1966]

04. It is against the law to come closer than one hundred meters from where a carcass of a dead whale is.

05. It is against the law to crush a can of beer between your breasts.

06. It is against the law to dress up as Batman or robin.

07. It is against the law to drive a cat or dog attached to a vehicle in a public place.

08. It is against the law to have an article of disguise without a lawful excuse.

09. It is against the law to leave the keys in the ignition or inside a vehicle of unattended vehicle.

10. It is against the law to roam the streets wearing black clothes, felt shoes, and black shoe polish on your face.

11. It is against the law to swim unless you are wearing a neck-to-knee swimsuit in Brighton Beach.

12. It is against the law to touch electric wires that cause death instantly.

13. It is against the law to walk on the right-hand side of a footpath.

14. Bars are required to stable, water, and feed the horses that come with patrons.

15. If you advertise a reward for finding lost or stolen objects, the advertisement must have a statement that no questions will be asked.

16. Men are allowed to cross-dress, just as long as their dresses are not strapless.

17. No man under 4ft 8 inch is allowed to surf on Klondike Beach (due to the size of the waves.)

18. Taxicabs are required to carry a bale of hay in their trunks.

19. The legal age for straight sex is 16 unless the person is in the care/custody of the older person, in which case it is 18.

20. Under Australian Communications Authority (ACA) regulations, a modem can't pick up on the first ring. If it does the ACA permit for your modem is invalid and there is a $12,000 fine. [Telecommunications Act 1991.]

21. *Melbourne*: Vacuuming your house between 10 pm and 7 am during weekdays and 10 pm and 9 am during the weekends is against the law.

22. *Queensland*: It is against the law to ask any person if their father was a criminal.

23. *Sydney*: It is against the law to throw a bag containing both cats and dogs into the Parramatta River. But it is okay to throw a bag of cats or a bag of dogs.

24. *Vermont*: A husband has to sign off in the event his wife needs dentures.

25. *Victoria*: It is against the law to wear hot pink pants afternoon on a Sunday.

26. *Victoria*: It is against the law to change a light bulb unless you're a licensed electrician.

****

02. Weird Laws -- Argentina

01. According to an Argentina ordinance, disc jockeys have to play as many tango records as all other types of music combined.

02. Featherbeds are illegal. It is believed the bed may encourage lustful feelings.

****

03. Weird Laws -- Bahrain

01. The law prohibits a male gynecologist from looking directly at a woman patient's organs; he must use mirror reflections to do his job.

****

04. Weird Laws -- Bangladesh

01. Children as young as 15 can be sent to jail for cheating on their annual exams.

02. You must not call any person over the age of 32 a "virgin" in case they become offended.

$$*****************$$

05. Weird Laws -- Barbados

01. Only members of the military are permitted to wear camouflage in Barbados, [The ban was enacted in the 1980s to prevent gang members from impersonating soldiers and robbing people]

$$*****************$$

06. Weird Laws -- Belgium

01. It is against the law for a pub to sell more than 25% of foreign beer.

02. It is against the law to insinuate that someone is Swedish.

03. A driver who needs to turn through oncoming traffic has the right of way unless he slows down or stops.

04. Sweepstakes is prohibited.

05. Until 1984 Belgians were made to choose their children's names from a list of 1500 drawn up in the days of Napoleon.

06. *Antwerp*: It is against the law to wear a red hat while walking down the main street.

07. *Brussels*: It is against the law for a girl to wear a mini skirt that is more than 4 inches above her knee without written permission from her father.

08. *Brussels*: It is LEGAL to throw Brussels sprouts at tourists.

****

07. Weird Laws -- Bolivia

01. *La Paz:* It is against the law for a married woman to drink more than one glass of wine when out at a bar or restaurant.

****

08. Weird Laws -- Brazil

01. *Noiva do Cordeiro:* It is against the law for men to live in this town. (This is an all-woman town and allows male residence as long as they follow their rules.)

02. *Rio Claro:* it is against the law to sell watermelons.

****

09. Weird Laws -- Burma

01. It is against the law for anyone to own a modem.

****

10. Weird Laws -- Cambodia

01. It is against the law to criticize the Khmer Rouge, the Heng Samrin, or Hun Sen regimes. [Violators will have their heads chopped off]

02. It is against the law to intentionally jump onto any of the 10 million land mines that scar the country.

03. It is against the law to use water pistols during New Year's celebrations. [However, the only punishment for breaking the rule is the confiscation of the water gun, nothing more.]

****

11. Weird Laws -- Canada

01. It is against the law for clear or non-dark sodas to contain caffeine.

02. It is against the law to kill a sick person by frightening them.

03. It is against the law to make burgers out of polar bears.

04. It is against the law to show public affection on Sunday.

05. It is against the law to watch or listen to an encrypted broadcast that is not licensed by the Canadian government.

06. It is illegal to protect the rear license plate by glass or plastic.

07. 35% of radio stations' content must be "Canadian Content".

08. According to Canadian law, "Everyone commits an offense who... (b) makes, prints, publishes, distributes, sells or has in his possession for publication, distribution or circulation a crime comic."

09. According to Canada's Currency Act, 1985, stores can legally refuse excessive amounts of coins. The maximum for nickels is $5.00 while for the looney (Canadian dollar coin worth $1.00) the maximum is $25.00.

10. By law your parents or grandparents must have come from France, Scotland, or Ireland.

11. Children must not be buried alive in snow deeper than six feet.

12. Citizens may not publicly remove bandages.

13. Comic books which depict any illegal acts are banned.

14. One out of every five songs on the radio must be sung by a Canadian.

15. Residents are not allowed to have an Internet connection faster than 56k.

16. You may not paint a ladder as it will be slippery when wet.

17. Alberta: Businesses must provide rails for tying up horses.

18. Alberta: It is against the law to set fire to the wooden leg of a wooden-legged man

19. Alberta: Wooden logs may not be painted.

20. Beaconsfield: It is against the law to have more than two colors of paint on your house.

21. Beaconsfield: You may not own a log or paper marche cabin.

22. Calgary, Alberta: it is against the law to buy and/or sell non-prescription contacts at costume shops

23. Cobourg: If you have a water trough in your front yard it must be filled by 5:00 a.m.

24. Etobicoke: No more than 3.5 inches of water is allowed in a bathtub.

25. Gananoque: Homeowners are responsible for clearing snow off municipal sidewalks in front of their house or business.

26. Kanata: The color of house and garage doors is regulated by city bylaws.

27. Kanata: You must not repair your car in the street.

28. Montreal: It is against the law to swear...in French.

29. Nova Scotia: According to Halifax's Regional Municipality Bylaws for Taxis and Limousines, number 42 a), drivers must wear shoes and socks. And it is against the law for them to wear T-shirts.

30. Oak Bay, B.C: If your parrot talks too loudly, you could be fined $100.

31. Ontario: It is against the law to carpool with someone unless you meet ALL of the following criteria: You can only travel from home to work (no rides to schools, hospitals, daycare, etc.). You cannot cross municipal boundaries (nor driving to the adjacent municipality for a GO station, TTC subway, airport, etc.). You must ride with the same driver each day. You must pay the driver weekly only. [Good News: These criteria must be met ONLY when you want to drive in the designated carpooling lanes on major highways, such as the Don Valley Parkway in southern Ontario.]

32. Ottawa: It is against the law to remove your feet from the pedals when bicycling.

33. Petrolia, Ontario: According to Article 3, 772.3.6, "Yelling, shouting, hooting, whistling or singing is prohibited at all times."

34. Quebec: All business signs must be predominantly in French.

35. Quebec: It is against the law to impersonate a foreigner.

36. Souris, Prince Edward Island: It's Illegal to Build Snowmen taller than 30 inches. (Souris is well-known for its curious 'Singing Sands' Beach.)

37. St. John's, Newfoundland: Trash bags must be at least 1.5 mm thick and hold between 25 and 90 liters.

38. St. Paul, Alberta: It is against the law for anyone 15 or younger to loiter in a public place without the supervision of a parent or guardian between 12:01 a.m. and 6 a.m.

****

12. Weird Laws -- China

01. It is against the law for a person if he fails to announce the approach of Russians.

02. It is against the law for adult children to not visit their parents "often".

03. It is against the law to bind a child's feet to stop them from growing.

04. It is against the law to eat another man's wife intentionally as part of a meal.

05. It is against the law to share the 'secret' of sericulture (silk-making) as per an ancient Chinese law.

06. It is against the law to store more than 1 ton of explosives (fireworks) in the cellar of a house.

07. It is against the law to use baby names that cannot be translated into Mandarin.

08. A person must be intelligent to go to college.

09. According to a statement issued by the State Administration for Religious Affairs in 2007, the law, which strictly stipulates the procedures by which one is to reincarnate, is "an important move to institutionalize management of reincarnation." China banned Buddhist monks in Tibet from reincarnating without government permission.

10. Every household can keep only one pet dog and that dog must be under 14 inches tall.

11. If you pass anyone over the age of 70 in the street, you must bow to them and say a prayer to the Gods of the Ancients.

12. Men who have been employed by the company for less than a year are forbidden from dating a colleague. Male workers under the age of 25 are not permitted to date a colleague at all. Women who have been employed for less than three months are forbidden from dating a colleague, and if they find a boyfriend who doesn't work at the company, he must be vetted by the management to make sure he is "suitable". However, if the salary of an employee is higher than 15,000 RMB per month, they are exempt from all rules.

13. The Jasmine Revolution in Tunisia inspired Chinese protestors, the government decided to ban the flower.

14. *Guizhou*: Children at Luoyang Elementary School are required by local law to stop and raise their hands to all cars which pass them on the street.

15. *Beijing*: It is against the law for drivers of power-driven vehicles to stop at a pedestrian crossing. [Source: Article 40 of the Beijing Traffic Laws].

16. *Shanghai:* It is against the law to own a red car.

****

13. Weird Laws – Costa Rica

01. You can drink alcohol while driving as long as your blood-alcohol level is not above 0.75 percent.

****

14. Weird Laws -- Cyprus

01. It is against the law to drink water whilst driving.

****

15. Weird Laws -- Denmark

01. It is against the law for restaurants to charge for water unless it is accompanied by another item such as ice or a lemon slice.

02. It is against the law for women to wear wigs.

03. It is against the law to carrying pepper spray.

04. It is against the law to eat raw bacon if there is a full moon.

05. It is against the law to not report when a person has died.

06. It is against the law to start your car without first checking to see if any children are sleeping under a car.

07. It is against the law to wear a mask.

08. Any carport added to a building increases the value of the building by 15.5 times the cost of building the carport.

09. Before starting your car you are required to check lights, brakes, steering, and honk your horn.

10. Headlights must be on whenever a vehicle is being operated to distinguish it from parked cars.

11. If a horse-drawn carriage is trying to pass a car and the horse becomes uneasy, the owner of the car is required to pull over.

12. If your vehicle breaks down and you leave it on the side of the road, you must mark the vehicle with a red, reflecting triangle.

13. In restaurants, you don't have to pay for your food unless, in your own opinion, you are 'full' at the end of your meal. If not, you can proceed without paying the bill at all.

14. It is not illegal for a convicted prisoner to escape from prison. If the escapee is caught, he only serves the rest of his sentence.

15. No man may say to his wife that she is "uglier than her mother". The penalty is up to 1 year in prison.

16. There are 24,000 approved government names that parents can choose from. If they want a different name, they must apply for permission.

****

16. Weird Laws -- Egypt

01. It is against the law to look through binoculars near airports.

****

17. Weird Laws -- England

01. It is against the law for a lady to eat chocolates on a public conveyance.

02. It is against the law for a Member of Parliament to enter the House of Commons wearing armor.

03. It is against the law not to tell the taxman anything you don't want him to know - though you don't have to tell him anything you don't mind him knowing [Source: UK's Tax Avoidance Schemes Regulations 2006]

04. It is against the law to ask a Scotsman what he wears under his kilt.

05. It is against the law to be drunk on Licensed Premises (such as a pub or bar).

06. It is against the law to carry a plank along the pavement.

07. It is against the law to damage the grass.

08. It is against the law to die in the Houses of Parliament in England. [Repealed]

09. It is against the law to eat Mince pies on Christmas Day.

10. It is against the law to handle a salmon in suspicious circumstances.

11. It is against the law to hang a bed out of a window.

12. It is against the law to impersonate a Chelsea Pensioner.

13. It is against the law to import potatoes into England or Wales if you have reasonable cause to believe that they are Polish.

14. It is against the law to keep a lunatic with a license.

15. It is against the law to leave baggage unattended.

16. It is against the law to let your pet mate with any pet from the royal house.

17. It is against the law to pick up abandoned baggage. It is assumed as an act of terrorism and theft.

18. All land must be left to the eldest son.

19. All males over the age of 14 must carry out 2 or so hours of longbow practice a week supervised by the local clergy.

20. Committing suicide is classified as a capital crime.

21. If a steam locomotive is driven on roads, a man must walk in front of the vehicle with a red flag during the day and a red lantern at night to warn passers-by.

22. In 1888, a law was passed which stated that every cyclist had to constantly ring the bell on his bicycle non-stop while the machine was moving.

23. Interfering with the mail or sleeping with the consort of the Queen is classed as treason, and as such, carries the death penalty.

24. It is a treasonable offense to make any suggestions that the Monarchy was in any way involved in the death of Princess Diana.

25. It is an act of treason to place a postage stamp bearing the British monarch upside-down.

26. It is LEGAL for a male to urinate in public if he aims for his car's rear wheel and keeps his right hand on his vehicle.

27. No cows may be driven down the roadway between 10 AM and 7 PM unless there is prior approval from the Commissioner of Police. [Metropolitan Streets Act of 1867]

28. On the call "Bring out your dead" any family member who has died from the Black Plague must immediately be removed from the house to be carted away.

29. Only the Queen of England can eat the mute swan. If you are caught eating one, you may be fined or face prison-term.

30. Pregnant women are allowed to deliver their babies in any public place. They can legally relieve herself anywhere she wants – even, in a policeman's helmet.
31. Steam locomotives are restricted to a speed of 4 mph on roads.

32. The Prohibition and Inspections Act of 1998 forbids causing a nuclear explosion.

33. The head of any dead whale found on the British coast is legally the property of the King (monarch). The tail, on the other hand, belongs to the Queen.

34. Those wishing to purchase a television must also buy a license.

35. except for carrots, most goods may not be sold on Sunday.

36. *Blackpool:* It is against the law to fall off the top of Blackpool Tower - under any circumstance.

37. *London:* All double-decker buses must be painted red.

38. *London:* Companies may vote in local elections.

39. *London:* Freemen of the city of London (Those who have had the honor of the freedom of the city bestowed upon them) have the right to herd their cattle on any of London's bridges.

40. *London:* It is against the law for a cab to carry rabid dogs or corpses.

41. *London:* It is against the law to flag down a taxi if you have the plague.

42. *London:* It is against the law to throw a stick for your dog or use a camera tripod in any park.

43. *York:* it is legal to kill a Scotsman within the ancient city walls, but only if he is carrying a bow and arrow.

****

18. <u>Weird</u> <u>Laws</u> -- <u>Finland</u>

01. It is against the law to play music in a taxi without an appropriate license. They must pay royalties if they play music in their cars for paying customers.

02. Everyone has to pay a television tax whether they own one or not.

03. The government of Finland collects a "candy tax" for goods containing sugar. Bottled water gets taxed, but cookies do not.

04. Traffic fines are calculated as a percentage of the offender's most-recently-reported income.

05. Underground power lines and overhead power lines can't be by the roadside at the same time, they can only be placed at the roadside alone.

****

19. Weird Laws -- France

01. It is against the law to call a pig Napoleon, out of respect for Napoleon Bonaparte.
02. If an athlete doesn't play for the national team he/she can be banned from playing for his/her club.

03. It is against the law to die unless a cemetery plot has first been bought.

04. It is against the law to shoot Englishmen as they cross the English Channel towards France - unless they are sailing in a "boat of war".

05. It is against the law to take photos of police officers or police vehicles, even if they are just in the background.

06. It is against the law to use ketchup in school cafeterias.

07. According to a 1910 ban, kissing on train platforms is illegal. This law was made to help prevent rail delays.

08. Between the hours of 8 AM and 8 PM, 70% of the music played on the radio must be by French artists.

09. Drivers are legally required to carry a portable Breathalyzer in their vehicle.

10. In advertisements for products that contain salt or sugar, it is mandatory to mention that you should exercise and eat at least five fruits and vegetables a day.

11. Stores can only sell dolls with human faces; alien faces are prohibited.

12. You can legally marry a dead person as long as preliminary civic formalities have been completed which show that you and your fiancé/fiancée had planned to marry before your fiancé/fiancée died.

13. *Paris:* Any man carrying onions must be given the right of way in the streets.

14. *Paris:* Criminals can apply for sanctuary in Notre Dame Catherdral and must be "fed and watered" for up to six weeks.

****

20. Weird Laws -- Germany

01. It is against the law for a car to run out of gas on the Autobahn.

02. It is against the law to deny a chimney sweep access to your home if he demands it.

03. It is against the law to have the ashes of your loved one stored in an urn at home after cremation.

04. It is against the law to mention the date 1966 in any football ground.

05. It is against the law to ride a bicycle while drunk.

06. It is against the law to tune pianos at midnight.

07. It is against the law to wear a mask while on strike.

08. A pillow is classified as a "passive weapon" and hitting someone with one can lead to charges of assault.

09. An individual needs to get a license for fishing.

10. Every office must have a view of the sky, even if this is through a very small window.

11. *Munich:* By law, a pub can never be overcrowded - there is always room for one more drinker at each table - no matter how squashed people are.

12. *Munich:* During October Fest no person is ever legally drunk - no matter how much alcohol they have consumed.

****

21. Weird Laws -- Greece

01. It was against the law to wear a hat in the Olympic Stadium in ancient times as it would obstruct someone's view.

02. Couponing is against the law.

03. If anyone wants to get married, they need to publish their wedding notice in a newspaper (written in Greek) or on the City Hall notice board.

04. No one is allowed to play electronic games. [Source: Greek Law Number 3037]

05. Police are allowed to arrest anyone suspected of having HIV. They can force HIV testing, or publicize the names of HIV-positive people.

06. The Trojan War has not officially ended.

07. *Athens*: It is against the law to dance naked in the Acropolis.

****

22. Weird Laws – Hong Kong

01. "Singing of any song" on any 'bathing beach' is against the law unless you have written permission.

02. A visitor to Ocean Park may not use "obscene language", "fly a kite", use shoes "fitted with wheels" or "shout".

03. Dog keepers must apply for a dog license for keeping any dog over the age of 5 months. [Source: Rabies Regulation, Cap. 421A]

04. If a man cheats on his wife she is legally allowed to kill him but with only her bare hands.

05. Under the guise of 'public safety and 'public order, "a public procession consisting of more than 30 persons can only take place if the Police Commissioner has been notified a week in advance and the Commissioner has notified the organizer that he has no objection."

****

23. Weird Laws – Hungary

01. *Lorinc:* Cats can only be taken on the street if they are on a lead.

****

24. Weird Laws -- Iceland

01. It is against the law to run a Marathon (26-mile trek) in less than 3 hours 30 minutes.

02. It was once against the law to have a pet dog in a city in Iceland.

****

25. Weird Laws -- India

01. It is against the law to play music sound systems (decks, etc.) in wedding functions after 10:00 PM.

02. It is against the law to sell alcohol on Election Day.

03. It is against the law to set off fireworks after 10:00 PM.

04. A kite is considered as an 'aircraft'. You need a permit to make, possess or fly a kite. [Source: Indian Aircraft Act, 1934] However, this law has never been followed in India.

05. Alcohol laws are determined on a state-by-state basis. This simply means they decide whether to outlaw it entirely or to set a drinking age. The state of Gujarat and Bihar has completely banned it. In Maharashtra, anyone who wants to drink needs to be at 25-year-old. The minimum age for consuming alcohol is 18 in Goa, Himachal Pradesh, UP, Sikkim, and Puducherry.

06. Grocery stores, pharmacies, small and large retailers, or wholesalers cannot provide items in plastic carryout bags in some states of India. You may be liable to pay a hefty fine. In my home town Haldwani (District- Nainital, State-Uttarakhand), this law is being enforced strictly. City officials conduct searches from time to time at stores and even on fruit or vegetable carts and confiscate all Polly bags and impose hefty fines. In one particular case, a megastore was fined millions of INR. Carrying out the order of the Nainital High Court, city authorities imposed a fine of INR 500 (US$8) per plastic carry bag on that megastore. Thermocol has also been banned in my city.

07. If a man gets caught for hooking up with a married woman, he can get prosecuted for adultery, but the woman can't. [Indian Penal Code, 1860 (Section 497)]

08. It is against the law for train drivers to go toilet while driving trains. [They can relieve themselves only in 'next' station.]

09. It is mandatory to show your Identity card to use the Internet in cyber cafes.

10. It is strictly forbidden to use Red or Blue beacon light on private vehicles.

11. Killing King Cobra (a very poisonous snake) is against the law even if it bites you. You are not allowed to kill the one. [If you die from its poison, your kith and kin will be given compensation of INR 3,00,000 = around US$5000]

12. One of the criteria to become an Andhra Pradesh motor vehicle inspector is "well-brushed teeth". [Indian Motor Vehicles Act, 1914]

13. Playing cards for money is considered a form of gambling in India. Violators may be arrested immediately.

14. Probably the weirdest law of India -- According to Section 309 of the Indian Penal Code suicide is legal but not the attempt-to-suicide. If your suicidal attempt failed, you may be arrested. But if you die, then the person who directly or indirectly forced you for committing suicide may be booked in strict provisions of the Indian Penal Code.

15. To enforce the two-child policy in the state of Kerala, a penalty of INR10,000 (US$150) is imposed on parents who have a third child.

****

26. Weird Laws -- Indonesia

01. It is against the law to not flush the toilet after using it. Special police randomly check on public restrooms and violators are publicly caned.

02. No woman is allowed to be taller than her husband.

****

27. <u>Weird</u> <u>Laws</u> -- <u>Ireland</u>

01. It is against the law to be drunk in a pub. This law has rarely, if ever, been executed.

02. It is against the law to cross a railway track on a bicycle, whereas you can drive across it legally.

03. It is against the law to exercise any type of witchcraft, sorcery, or enchantment.

04. According to a 2006 law, "A person who carries out, or causes the carrying out of, a nuclear explosion in the State shall be guilty of an offense."

05. If a Leprechaun (a creature, like a little man, with magic powers) calls at your door you must, by law, give him a share of your dinner.

06. The Tippling Act 1735 prohibits a publican from pursuing a customer for money owed for any drink given on credit.

07. You can drive around on public roads without ever proving your competency at driving.

****

28. <u>Weird</u> <u>Laws</u> -- <u>Israel</u>

01. It is against the law for a chicken to lay an egg on Friday or Saturday.

02. It is against the law to bring bears to the beach.

03. It is against the law to ride bicycles without a license.

04. If you have been operating an illegal radio station for five or more years, the station becomes legal.

05. It is a criminal offense, punishable by death, to deface the HaKotel Hama"aravi (Wailing Wall).

06. No loud voices or bright lights are allowed during weekends.

07. Raising a pig on Israeli soil will result in the killing of said pig.

08. *Arad:* It is against the law to feed animals in public places.

09. *Arad:* It is against the law to operate a mobile spay/neuter clinic - it is considered peddling.

10. *Haifa:* It is against the law to take bears or very fat women onto the beach.

11. *Ramat-Hasharon:* It is against the law to raise Rottweiler dogs.

12. *Sabbath:* It is against the law to pick your nose.

****

29. Weird Laws -- Italy

01. It is against the law for a man to wear a skirt.

02. It is against the law for obese people to wear polyester.

03. It is against the law to die in the Italian village of Falciano del Massico.

04. It is against the law to drive through a historic zone (Zona Traffico Limitata) without a special permit.

05. It is against the law to eat and drink on prehistoric sites.

06. It is against the law to make coffins out of anything except nutshells or wood.

07. It is against the law to practice the profession of charlatanry.

08. It is a felony to strike someone with a fist.

09. *Florence:* It is against the law to attach padlocks to any public statute or building.

10. It is against the law to sit on steps and courtyards or to eat and drink in the immediate vicinity of churches and public buildings in Florence.

11. *Milan:* it is a legal requirement to smile at all times, except during funerals or hospital visits.

12. *Reggio Emilia:* According to a city law if a pet shares a meal, it must be given equal portions.

13. *Rome:* It is against the law for a man to bare his chest in public.

14. *Turin:* Dog owners must take their dogs on a walk at least three times a day.

****

30. Weird Laws -- Japan

01. It is against the law to carry out the death sentence on holidays, the end of the year, and the New Year.

02. It is against the law to cook Fugu (Blow Fish) for more than 80 seconds. Fugu contains deadly poison in the organs. Despite the risk, fugu dishes are considered special feasts in Japan.

03. It is against the law to damage or throw away money. Violators could be fined up to ¥200,000 or spend a year in prison.

04. It is against the law to drive through a puddle and splash a pedestrian.

05. Every man and woman aged 40 and over must not have a waist measuring over 32 inches and 36 inches respectively. There is no penalty or punishment in law. It is aimed at putting pressure on local governments and companies.

06. Home brewed liquor with more than 1% alcohol is illegal.

07. If an older brother asks to marry your girlfriend, by law and honor you, and your girlfriend, must agree.

08. If the driver of the car is intoxicated, the passenger, also, can be booked.

09. The Nationality Law says that a child born out of wedlock to a non-Japanese mother is only recognized as a citizen if the Japanese father admits paternity before the child's birth or marries the mother before the child turns 20.

10. Those engaged in campaigning for an election can be reimbursed up to ¥12,000 for hotel stays, ¥3,000 for food, and ¥500 for snacks per day.

11. Under the Law for Temporary Measures concerning Fines (Penal Provisions Related to Treatment of Explosives), an individual can be fined up to ¥10,000 for not reporting an explosive to the police.

12. War is against the law in Japan.

13. Women who get divorced must wait six months before marrying again. If a woman gives birth to a child during these six months, that child is legally her ex-husband's.

✱✱✱✱✱✱✱✱✱✱✱✱✱✱✱✱✱✱✱

31. Weird Laws -- Kenya

01. *Nairobi:* All buildings must be painted every year.

02. *Nairobi:* Failure to a fence or fencing your land 'inappropriately' is illegal.

03. *Nairobi:* If there are more than six passengers at a terminus, then they must stand in a queue.

****

32. Weird Laws – Korea (North)

01. It is against the law for tourists to leave the hotel at night under any circumstances.

02. It is against the law for tourists to roam the streets alone. They must be accompanied by their Korean guides at all times.

03. It is against the law to bring books or other written material in the Korean language, including anything with religious content.

04. It is against the law to fold the newspaper or throw it away if there is a picture of a leader on it.

05. It is against the law to own a private vehicle. [Government officials are exempted]

06. Any technology incorporating Global Positioning Systems must be left with North Korean customs on entry into the country and collected on departure.

07. Contraceptives and all religious materials, such as the bible and the Qur'an are banned.

08. Foreign mobile phones can be brought into the country but must be registered at the airport. They can only be used in North Korea by purchasing a North Korean SIM card.

09. Tourists are not allowed to use the local currency, the North Korean 'won,' and must instead use either Euro, US Dollars, or the Chinese Yuan.

10. You are legally bound to bow and keep your hands by your side and not behind your back when you come up to a statue of the top leaders.

11. You cannot wear black jeans as they are linked to the United States. If you are going to wear denim, it must be blue.

****

33. Weird Laws – Korea (South)

01. A person has the "right" to commit violence in so far as he can afford to pay for the damages.

02. All dogs sold for consumption must have a government-approved tattoo.

03. It is against the law to eat stray cats.

04. It is against the law to impersonate an animal while in a restaurant.

05. Traffic police are obligated to report to their supervisors the bribes they received for the day because that stops it from happening.

****

34. Weird Laws -- Lebanon

01. Homosexual bestiality is a sin. Any man may legally have sex with a female animal. If they are caught having sex with a male animal, though, the penalty is death.

****

35. Weird Laws -- Maldives

01. Public observance of any religion other than Islam is prohibited. It is against the law to import bibles into the country.

****

36. Weird Laws -- Mexico

01. It is against the law for clergymen to appear in public wearing their religious garb.

02. It is against the law to take your feet off the pedals when you are riding a bike.

03. It is against the law to throw fireworks by hand during Holy Week.

04. All males must wear trousers, and such groups of employees as hack drivers and newspaper delivery boys must adopt uniforms.

05. Any kind of nude artistic display is illegal.

06. Boneshakers, safety bicycles, and any other similar machines are banned from the center of town.

07. During Holy Week, no horses or wheeled transport is allowed in the city.

08. If a Mexican enters the USA illegally it then becomes illegal for him to return to Mexico.

09. *Guadalajara:* It is against the law to shout offensive words in any public place.

10. *Guadalajara:* Women who work for the government of the city may not wear miniskirts or any other "provocative" garment during office hours.

11. *Mexico City:* It is against the law to say to anyone "Have a nice day."

****

37. <u>Weird</u> <u>Laws</u> -- <u>Monaco</u>

01. It is mandatory for marriages to be announced in public. You are needed to scribble it on a piece of paper and stick it on the door of the Town Hall for a 10-day period that includes two Sundays.

****

38. <u>Weird</u> <u>Laws</u> -- <u>Morocco</u>

01. Anyone in company with someone who possesses narcotics, even if they are unaware that their companion has them, can be tried for the same crime.

02. Children over the age of 12 are prohibited from telling Knock-Knock jokes.

03. It is against the law to kill a mouse unless for consumption.

****

39. Weird Laws -- Netherlands

01. It is against the law to impersonate a blind person after dark.

02. It is against the law to urinate into a canal. [Pregnant women are exempted]

03. It is legal to smoke cannabis in public places but to smoke tobacco is illegal. You may carry up to 5 grams of marijuana.

04. Prostitution is legal but the prostitutes must pay taxes like any other business.

****

40. Weird Laws – New Zealand

01. You cannot let the cat leave your house unless it has three bells around its neck.

****

41. Weird Laws -- Nigeria

01. A person is not deemed to have killed another if the death of that other person does not take place within a year and a day of the cause of death. – [Source: Criminal Code Act]

02. An individual can go to court to seek an order preventing someone from going about claiming that he/she and that individual are married. [Source: Matrimonial Causes Act]

03. It is against the law to advertise a reward for the return of stolen or lost property and stating that no question will be asked. [Source: Criminal Code Act]

04. It is against the law to paint a private car in the color known colloquially as 'army green'. [Source: Army Colour (Prohibition of Use) Act]

05. It is against the law to represent himself/herself to be a witch or to have the power of witchcraft. Violators are liable to imprisonment for two years – [Source: Criminal Code Act]

06. It is against the law to take mineral water.

****

42. Weird Laws -- Norway

01. Fee is levied on each purchase of any plastic bottle which is returned upon return of the bottle.

02. Female dogs and cats can't be spayed. Only male dogs and cats can be neutered.

03. It is against the law to own television sets and VCRs. without license.

04. Prostitution is illegal, but being a prostitute is not.

****

43. Weird Laws -- Paraguay

01. Duelling is legal just as long as both parties are registered blood donors.

****

44. Weird Laws -- Philippines

01. It is against the law to be cremated with a living creature in a pocket of your clothing.

02. A girl must avert her eyes from her father when she speaks to him.

03. Some time back, based on the number of the car license plate, cars were restricted from use on certain days of the week. To be able to drive every day of the week you were needed to own 4 cars.

04. the Philippines is one of the two countries divorce is against the law [the Vatican is another country where divorce is illegal]

05. Trespassers who disregard property rights cannot be made to move out and their illegal structures cannot be demolished without the landowner finding a relocation site for them and paying them first!!!

****

45. Weird Laws -- Portugal

01. It is against the law to urinate in the ocean.

****

46. Weird Laws -- Romania

01. In the 1980s, President Nicolae Ceausescu banned the game of Scrabble, describing it as "overly intellectual" and a "subversive evil."

02. Mickey Mouse was banned in 1935 because of fears that the sight of a 10ft high rodent on-screen would terrify the nation's children.

****

47. Weird Laws -- Russia

01. It is against the law to brush your teeth more than twice a day.

02. It is against the law to get caught cheating in an exam.

03. It is against the law to say any sentence containing more than four words in English.

04. It is against the law to tell kids that gay people exist.

05. It is mandatory to be willing to work 16 hours a day or face imprisonment.

06. Some areas of the country have laws that require all boys in the area to have the middle name of "Stalin."

07. Moscow weathermen can be fined for inaccurate forecasts.

08. *Chelyabinsk:* It is against the law to drive a dirty car.

****

48. Weird Laws -- Samoa

01. It is against the law to forget your wife's birthday.

****

49. Weird Laws – Saudi Arabia

01. It is against the law for non-Muslims to worship in public. If anyone converts from Islam or abandons religion, they face the death penalty.

02. It is against the law for a woman to drive a vehicle.

03. It is against the law to import any books featuring Christian symbols such as a cross.

04. It is against the law to possess any type of alcoholic beverage.

05. It is against the law to sell or wear anything red on Valentine's Day.

06. All food entering the country must be "halal". It is a country that considers all its citizens to be Muslim.

07. If an oil field is found in your garden you must report it to the state before digging a borehole greater than 5000 feet.

08. It is considered an offense if a woman appears in public unless accompanied by a male relative or guardian.

09. It is illegal to share a hotel room with (or live with, for that matter) someone of the opposite sex unless you're married or closely related.

10. Male citizens of SAUDI ARABIA have been banned from marrying women from four countries — Pakistan, Bangladesh, Chad, and Myanmar.

11. Male doctors may not examine women, and women doctors cannot examine men.

12. There is no minimum age for marriage.

****

50. <u>Weird Laws -- Scotland</u>

01. It is against the law to be a drunk in possession of a cow.

02. It is against the law to fish on Sundays.

03. It is against the law to hunt haggis between 1st April and 30th July.

04. If someone knocks on your door and requires the use of your toilet, it is against the law to refuse them.

05. On Rabbie Burns night, 25th January, all Scottish people must eat Haggis, Neeps, and Tatties.

06. Trespassing on someone else's land is LEGAL.

07. You are presumed guilty until proven innocent for some crimes.

08. *Aberdeen:* Any man owning more than 12 sheep must prove that he is not a "pimp" (brothel owner)

09. *Glasgow:* Any person operating a Fish and Chip shop must provide Deep Fried Mars Bars as part of their menu.

****

51. Weird Laws -- Singapore

01. It is against the law to carry a Bible.

02. It is against the law to come within 50 meters of a pedestrian crossing marker on any street.

03. It is against the law to enter the country with cigarettes.

04. It is against the law to speak to a donkey in Chinese.

05. It is against the law to urinate in an elevator.

06. A person convicted of littering three times, will have to clean the streets on Sundays wearing a sign saying "I am a litter lout." This will then be broadcasted on the local news.

07. As it is considered pornographic, you may not walk around your home nude. [Source: Miscellaneous Offences (Public Order and Nuisance) Act (Chapter 184, 1997 Edition) Section 27A]

08. Bungee jumping is illegal.

09. Eating raw fish while lecturing on Science is illegal.

10. Failure to flush a public toilet after use may result in hefty fines. Penalty: $150

11. Under the "Regulation of Imports and Exports (Chewing Gum) Regulations, the import of chewing gum has been illegal in Singapore since 1992 due to the damage it caused to the public transit system. Selling or chewing non-medical chewing gum is illegal. Chewing gums with "therapeutic" purposes are allowed. For example, nicotine gum and sugar-free gum with dental health benefits are allowed. But throwing chewing gum to the ground is also illegal in Singapore. Those violating this rule may be fined up to $1000 for the first offense. A second offense costs $2000 and being forced to clean a public area of the city for a day. Third-time offenders have to clean the streets wearing a bib that reads "I'm a litterer."

12. You are not allowed to drink, eat or take a photo for your blog on the metro (MRT). You can't even take a sip of water. Penalty: < $500

****

52. <u>Weird</u> <u>Laws</u> – <u>South</u> <u>Africa</u>

01. In the days of apartheid, all people of color had to be indoors by 9 PM, at which time a siren was sounded.

02. It is mandatory to stop when herders signal that they need to cross the road with their goats, pigs, mules, ass, horses, or other animals.

03. Men are not allowed to have intimate relations with girls younger than 18 years of age unless the man has more than $50, a sheep, and 3 bottles of gin since this is the fine that a man must pay for impregnating an underage girl.

04. You need a license to buy a television.

05. Young people wearing bathing suits are prohibited from sitting less than 12 inches apart.

****

53. <u>Weird Laws -- Spain</u>

01. It is against the law to drive without a spare pair of spectacles in the car.

02. It is against the law to wear swimming attire on public streets in Barcelona.

03. *Seville:* in 1983, an Alsatian dog was arrested for snatching handbags from shoppers.

****

54. <u>Weird Laws -- Swaziland</u>

01. It is against the law for young women to shake hands with older men.

02. Any woman who wears pants faces a possible punishment of having the pants ripped off and torn to pieces by soldiers.

03. Teenage girls were forbidden to make physical relations for 5 years to prevent AIDS.

✳✳✳✳✳✳✳✳✳✳✳✳✳✳✳✳✳✳

55. <u>Weird Laws -- Sweden</u>

01. It is against the law to be found buying the services of a prostitute, even though prostitution is legal.

02. It is against the law to paint your house without first getting a license.

03. A prince or princess, who marries without the consent of the government, forfeits the right of succession for his/her children and all other descendants.

04. According to a law that dogs attending a day-care center must be able to see out of a sunny window.

05. During the long hours of winter darkness it is against the law to complain that you wish it were sunny.

06. If you release pigs into an acorn wood (or a beechnutwood) mutually owned by you and at least one more, and exceeded your quota of allowed pigs, you will have to pay a fine for each pig to the other owners and to restore any damages caused by the extra pigs.

07. It is mandatory to keep your headlights on 24 hours a day.

08. Spanking is illegal in the classroom as well as at home.

09. Your rights to any ground that you own is only to the depth of half a meter.

****

56. Weird Laws -- Switzerland

01. It is against the law for a man to relieve himself while standing up, after 10 P.M.

02. It is against the law for any man to unilaterally declare war on another country.

03. It is against the law for banks to refuse vault owners to store dead relatives in their vaults - provided the period of storage does not exceed 7 months.

04. It is against the law to flush the toilet after 10 P.M. in an apartment building. The government considers it noise pollution.

05. It is against the law to hang clothes to dry, wash cars, or mow your lawn on Sunday.

06. It is against the law to leave your car keys inside the car with the door unlocked and open.

07. It is against the law to produce, store, sell and trade absinth, whereas it is legal to consume it.

08. It is against the law to ski down a mounting while reciting poetry.

09. At one time it was against the law to slam car doors in Switzerland.

10. It is required that every car with snow tires has to have a sticker on its dashboard which tells that the driver should not drive faster than 160 km/h with these tires.

11. People must pass verbal and written tests before they are allowed to own a dog.

****

57. Weird Laws -- Thailand

01. It is against the law to buy alcohol between midnight to 11 A.M. and 2 P.M. to 5 P.M.

02. It is against the law to drive a vehicle while not wearing a shirt

03. It is against the law to leave your house if you are not wearing underwear.

04. It is against the law to step on the local money or coins. [All the bills and coins in Thailand have a picture of the King printed on them. As the King is highly revered, stepping on his likeness can not only get you landed in jail but can also lead to a serious beating.]

05. It is against the law to throw chewed bubble gum onto the sidewalk.

06. At the age of thirty, unmarried women become the property of the state.

****

58. Weird Laws -- Turkey

01. It is against the law for men over the age of 80 to become pilots.

02. It is against the law to fall in love with a neighbors' son, daughter, wife, servant, or any of his animals.

03. It was against the law to drink coffee during the 16th and 17th centuries. It was punishable by death.

04. It is mandatory to have a reflective early warning device, a fire extinguisher, and a first aid kit in the vehicle.

05. Married women are forbidden from taking a job unless they have their husbands' consent.

06. Stealing olives before they are ripe can result in a jail sentence of up to 2 years.

****

59. Weird Laws -- UAE

01. It is against the law to display affection (kissing, hugging, holding hands) publicly.

02. No person (including foreign tourists) is allowed to eat, or drink in a public place during the day of Ramadan.

****

60. WEIRD LAWS -- the USA

If you reside in California, Colorado, Texas, and are in the armed forces, there is a legal provision for proxy marriages. In proxy marriage, either the bride or the groom is present during the wedding ceremony. The absent party can be represented by a proxy (your friend, acquaintance, etc.). In Montana, this rule is even more relaxed. Here both the bride and the groom can be represented by another person. This is called a 'double proxy marriage'

Following Are State-wise Weird laws in the USA--

60--*01.* <u>Weird</u> <u>Laws</u> -- <u>Alabama</u>

01. It is against the law to maim one's self to escape duty. [Source: Section 13A-14-1 of Alabama Code]

02. It is against the law to play Dominoes on Sunday. [Source: Section 13A-12-1 of Alabama Code]

03. All property of the wife, held by her previous to the marriage or to which she may become entitled after the marriage in any manner, is the separate property of the wife and is not subject to the liabilities of the husband. [Source: Section 30-4-1 of Alabama Code]

04. Fraudulently pretending to be a clergyman is illegal. [Source: Section 13A-14-4 of Alabama Code]

05. Issue of incestuous marriages not deemed illegitimate. [Source: Section 30-1-3 of Alabama Code]

06. Only 5 minutes are allowed for an individual to vote. [Source: Section 17-9-13 of Alabama Code]

07. *City- Mobile:* Fortunetellers need a permit to tell fortune to somebody. [Source: Sec. 23-1]

08. *City- Mobile:* It is against the law for any person to possess confetti in some cities. [Source: Sec. 39-77.]

****

60--*02.* Weird Laws -- Alaska

01. *City- Anchorage*: It is against the law to tie their pet dog to the roof of a car. [Source: Section 9.36.150]

02. *City- Anchorage*: It is against the law to throw or deposit upon any street any glass bottle, glass, nails, tacks, wire, cans, or any other substance likely to injure any person, animal, or vehicle upon such street. [Source: Section 9.36.100]

03. *City- Haines*: It is against the law to permit a drunken person to sell or serve alcoholic beverages. [Source: Section 9.04.030]

04. *City- Juneau*: It is against the law for an animal owner to let their pet into barbershops. [Source: Section 36.25.010]

05. *City- Nome*: It is against the law to roam with bow and arrow, or slingshot within the city. [Source: 13.25.050]

****

60--*03.* Weird Laws -- Arizona

01. It is against the law to manufacture imitation cocaine. [Source – Section 13-3453]

02. *City Tempe:* You must be 18 years old to buy spray paint. [Source: Sec. 22-103]

****

60--04. <u>Weird Laws</u> -- <u>Arkansas</u>

01. It's prohibited to pronounce "Arkansas" incorrectly. "It should be pronounced in three (3) syllables, with the final 's' silent, the 'a' in each syllable with the Italian sound, and the accent on the first and last syllables. The pronunciation with the accent on the second syllable with the sound of 'a' in "man" and the sounding of the terminal 's' is an innovation to be discouraged." In simple words, you should pronounce it as **ar-kan-saw**. [Source: Arkansas Code 1-4-105]

02. *City- Little Rock:* It is against the law to sound the horn on a vehicle at any place where cold drinks or sandwiches are served after 9:00 p.m. [Source: Sec. 18-54]

****

60--05. Weird Laws -- California

01. *City- Cathedral City:* It is against the law to sleep in an automobile or other vehicle parked on any sidewalk, street, alley, or other public places, including any approved private street or right-of-way. [Source: 11.04.030]

02. *City- Chico:* It is against the law for any person in the city, to play baseball or any other game upon any street, sidewalk, lane, or alley. [Source: 9.26.010]

03. *City- Eureka:* It is against the law to lie or sleep on any sidewalk, street, alley, or other public places in the city. [Source: 130.02]

04. *City- Walnut:* It is against the law to wear a mask or disguise on a public street without a permit from the sheriff. [Source: Law about "Mask or disguise—Wearing"]

05. *City- Walnut:* It is against the law for any person to fly, above an altitude of ten feet above the ground, or near any electrical conductive public utility wires or facilities, any kite or balloon which has a body or any parts, tail, string or ribbon. [Source: Law about "Kite flying restricted"]

****

60--06. Weird Laws -- Colorado

01. *City- Alamosa:* Any person owning, keeping, harboring, or having custody of any dog or potbelly pig over three (3) months of age within the city must obtain a license. [Source: Sec. 3-46]

02. *City- Alamosa:* It is against the law for any person to knowingly project any missile at or against any vehicle or equipment designed for the transportation of persons or property. [Source: Sec. 11-50]

03. *City- Louisville:* It is unlawful for any person to maintain or to keep any cattle, sheep, goats, swine, chickens, horses, or other livestock within the city. [Source: Sec. 6.16.020]

****

60--07. Weird Laws -- Connecticut

01. It is against the law to hunt or discharges any firearm from any public highway shall be fined. [Source: Sec. 53-204]

02. Town or probate records shall not be kept in any room in which alcoholic liquor is sold. [Source: Sec. 30-97]

****

60--*08.* Weird Laws -- Delaware

01. *Rehoboth Beach:* It is against the law to disrobe under the boardwalk, on the beach, or in any vehicle or truck while such vehicle is parked upon any public street or way or other public places in plain view of the public. [Source: Section 198-14]

****

60--*09.* Weird Laws -- Florida

01. It is against the law for any person to confine a pig during pregnancy in a cage. [Source: Article X, Section 19]

02. Doors of all public buildings must open outwards. [Source: Sec. 823.06]

03. *City- Daytona Beach:* It is against the law for any person, either as the owner, occupant, lessee, agent, tenant, or otherwise, to store or deposit, or cause or permit to be stored or deposited, any abandoned, junked or discarded motor vehicle or motor vehicles upon any public or private property within the city. [Source: Sec. 22-44]

04. *City- Destin:* No person in any city cemetery shall expose or offer for sale any article or thing, nor shall he station or place any stand, cart, or vehicle for the transportation, sale, or display of any such article or thing. [Source: Sec. 7-34]

05. *City- Destin:* It is unlawful and a civil infraction for any dog or cat, when unprovoked, to approach or chase any person in an apparent attitude of attack or a vicious or terrorizing manner. [Source: Sec. 4-8]

06. *City- Miami Beach:* It is prohibited for any person to have in his possession, control, management, or custody any swine within the city. [Source: Sec. 10-7]

****

60--*10.* Weird Laws -- Georgia

01. *City- Athens-Clarke County:* It is against the law for the owner or keeper of any hog, cattle, mule, sheep, goat, fowl, or any other livestock or nontraditional livestock animal to permit it to run at large within the limits of Athens-Clarke County or to stray from the property of the owner or keeper or to go upon the premises of any other person. [Source: Sec. 4-1-5.]

02. *City- Athens-Clarke County:* No person in Athens-Clarke County shall give away any live animal, fish, reptile, or bird as a prize for, or as an inducement to enter, any contest, game, or other competition [Source: Sec. 4-1-9]

03. *City- Columbus:* It is unlawful and disorderly conduct for any person to tease or harass, either by words, signs, or acts, on the streets or public places in the city any simple-minded, idiotic, or crazy person [Source: Sec. 14-34]

04. *City- Columbus:* It is against the law to wear a hat or any other covering of the head which obstructs the view of other persons, in any theater. [Source: Sec. 14-28]

05. *City- Conyers:* No person shall place any dead animal upon his premises or upon the premises of any other person, or allow any dead animal to remain upon his premises or permit any dead animal belonging to the person to remain upon the premises of another. [Source: Sec. 11-3-7]

06. *City- Dublin:* It is against the law to throw any object at a bird. [Source: Sec. 5-1]

07. *City- Kennesaw:* Every head of household is required to maintain a firearm together with ammunition. [Source: Sec 34-1a]

08. *City- Quitman:* It is against the law for a chicken to cross the road.

****

60--*11.* Weird Laws -- Hawaii

01. If getting more alcoholic drinks, the bartender must ask "who is that other drink (or drinks) for," and the customer must point them out. And that person (or persons) may not be holding a drink.

02. *City- Honolulu:* it is illegal to sing loudly outside after sunset.

****

60--*12.* Weird Laws -- Idaho

01. *City- Eagle:* It is against the law to sweep any dirt, trash, or rubbish from the interior of any building in the city onto any street, alley, or sidewalk in the city. [Source: Section- 5-2-2]

****

60--13. Weird Laws -- Illinois

01. An Individual under the age of 18 is allowed to get a gun permit with their parent or guardian's consent - even an infant!

02. *City- Galesburg:* It is against the law for a rider of a bicycle to remove both hands from the handlebars, or feet from the pedals, or practice any acrobatic or fancy riding on any street. [Source: Sec. 28-345]

03. *City- Galesburg:* It is against the law to keep or maintain any animal, poultry, or fowl in such a manner to cause inconvenience or disturbance to other persons because of noise, odor, or other cause. [Source: Sec. 4-6]

****

60--14. Weird Laws -- Indiana

01. It is against the law to catch a fish with bare hands. [Source: IC 14-22-9-1]

02. No paper or rag collecting shall be permitted at any time of the day or night on Sundays or legal holidays. [Source: Sec. 401-103]

03. *City- Indianapolis:* It is against the law to drive ride any horse on any street in the city at a speed above ten (10) miles per hour. [Source: Sec. 441-105]

04. *City- Warsaw:* It shall be unlawful for any person to throw any snowball, stone, or other hard substance, or any other missile along, across, or over any street. [Source: Sec. 54-61]

****

60--*15.* Weird Laws -- Iowa

01. The standard size for all boxes used in picking hops shall be 36 inches long, 18 inches wide, and 23 1/4 inches deep, inside measure. [Source: Section 4]

02. *City: Cedar Rapids:* It is against the law to tell fortunes or practice phrenology, palmistry, or clairvoyance in the city. [Source: 61.25]

****

60--16. Weird Laws -- Kansas

01. *City- Derby:* It is against the law for any person or persons, while operating a motor vehicle on the streets or highways of the city, to accelerate or speed the vehicle in such a manner or to turn a corner in such a manner as to cause the tires to screech. [Source: 10.12.010]

02. *City- Topeka:* No driver of a vehicle except a police car or other authorized emergency vehicle shall drive between the vehicles or persons comprising a parade when such vehicles or persons are in motion and are conspicuously designated as a parade.

03. *City- Wichita:* It is against the law to remove any dirt or earth from or place any dirt or earth on any of the streets, alleys, or other public grounds, including the public parks of the city and the airport, without first having obtained a permit from the director of public works or the board of park commissioners.

****

60--17. Weird Laws -- Kentucky

01. It is against the law for a woman to remarry the same man more than three times.

02. It is against the law to sell, exchange, offer to sell or exchange, display, or possess living baby chicks, ducklings, or other fowl or rabbits which have been dyed or colored.

03. *City- Louisville:* It is against the law to walk down a street, public or private, with an ice cream cone in your back pocket.

****

60--*18.* <u>Weird</u> <u>Laws</u> <u>--</u> <u>Louisiana</u>

01. It is against the law to curse firefighters while they are performing their duties.

02. It is against the law to ingest human or animal blood or human or animal waste.

03. It is against the law to intentionally place an order for any goods or services to be supplied or delivered to another person without his/her permission.

****

60--19. Weird Laws -- Maine

01. *City- Biddeford:* No person shall ride a bicycle upon any public sidewalk in the city. No person shall skate on any sidewalk in the city. [Source: Sec. 61-58]

02. *City- Freeport:* A person shall not sell or supply (including online retail) mercury fever thermometers to consumers and patients, except by prescription.

****

60--20. Weird Laws -- Maryland

01. City- Baltimore: It is against the law to take a lion into a cinema. Naturally.

02. City- Rockville: It is against the law for a person to wade or otherwise immerse any part of his body in any city-owned fountain or pool, except in pools constructed, operated, and maintained for the purpose of swimming. [Source: Sec. 13-64]

****

60--21. Weird Laws -- Massachusetts

01. It is against the law to engage in or promote a public/private boxing match or sparring exhibition, for which the contestants have received or have been promised any pecuniary reward, remuneration, or consideration.

****

60--22. Weird Laws -- Michigan

01. It is against the law to use high altitude decompression chamber or electrocution for killing dogs and other animals.

****

60--23. Weird Laws -- Minnesota

01. It is against the law to use park property for starting or landing of aircraft. [Source: Sec. 7-3-3]

****

60--24. Weird Laws -- Mississippi

01. An individual can become the natural parent of an illegitimate child only once. It is against the law to become the natural parent of an illegitimate child a second time.

****

60--25. Weird Laws -- Missouri

01. Yellow margarine is illegal.

02. *City- University City:* It is against the law for any person to offer for sale household goods in a "yard" or "garage" sale in an area in front of the front building line of the premises in which such person reside. It is also unlawful for any person to offer for sale household goods in a "yard" or "garage" sale more than two days during any calendar year. [Source: 9.28.060]

****

60--26. Weird Laws -- Montana

01. It is against the law for any person to sell, offer for sale, harbor, raise, or give away rats as pets, toys, premiums, novelties, or for any other purpose except as feed for reptiles or birds of prey or both. [Sec. 4-304]

****

60--27. Weird Laws -- Nebraska

01. The driver of a motor vehicle traveling on mountain highways shall hold such motor vehicle under control and as near the right-hand edge of the highway as reasonably possible. [Note: No mountain highways exist in Nebraska]

****

60--28. Weird Laws -- Nevada

01. City- Reno: It is against the law for any person to carry on, conduct, or maintain any marathon dancing or marathon walking.

02. City- Reno: It is against the law to place or maintains any chair, bench, or permanent seat on any street, alley, or sidewalk. [Source: Sec. 8.12.045]

****

60--29. Weird Laws -- New Hampshire

01. It is against the law to use a false or fictitious name to check into a hotel.

****

60--30. Weird Laws -- New Jersy

01. It is against the law to sell handcuffs to a person under 18 years of age. [Source: Sec. 2C:39-9.2]

02. It is against the law to wear a bullet-proof vest while engaged in the commission of, or an attempt to commit, or flight after committing or attempting to commit murder, manslaughter, robbery, burglary, kidnapping, criminal escape, or assault. [Source: Sec. 2C:39-13]

****

60--*31.* Weird Laws -- New Mexico

01. Riding a bicycle or hunting is expressly prohibited within the confines of the cemetery premises. [Source: Sec. 8-4-3]

****

62--*32.* Weird Laws -- New York

01. It is against the law to throw a ball at someone's head for fun.

02. It is against the law to do a puppet show in a window

03. Jumping off a building is punishable by death.

04. *City- Ocean City:* It is against the law to slurp their soup.

****

62--*33.* Weird Laws -- North Carolina

01. It is against the law to loiter on or near the premises of any jail or police station for any purpose during the hours of darkness.

02. A privilege tax is imposed on a white goods retailer at a flat rate for each new white good that is sold by the retailer.

****

60--*34.* Weird Laws -- North Dakota

01. It is against the law to lie down and fall asleep with your shoes on.

****

60--*35.* Weird Laws -- Ohio

01. It is against the law to erect or maintain any fence charged with electrical current.

02. *City- Cleveland:* A hunting license is required to catch mice.

****

60--36. Weird Laws -- Oklahoma

01. *City- Bartlesville:* It is against the law for any person, firm, or corporation that owns, leases, or controls any premises within the city to maintain on said premises more than a total of two (2) dogs and two (2) cats over the age of six (6) months outside of the primary dwelling unit. [Source: Section 3-25]

02. *City- Oklahoma City:* It is against the law to possess a stink bomb.

****

60--37. Weird Laws -- Oregon

01. It is against the law to leave a door open on the side of a vehicle available to traffic, or to pedestrians or bicycles on sidewalks or shoulders for a period of time longer than necessary to load or unload passengers. [Source: 811.490]

02. *City- Portland:* It is against the law for any person riding upon any vehicle, sled, or other conveyance to hitch or hold on to any part of another vehicle or conveyance to be propelled or drawn along any street or highway within the City. [Source: 16.70.520]

****

60--*38.* Weird Laws -- Pennsylvania

01. *City- Bensalem:* It is against the law for any club or person to advertise the prizes or their dollar value to be awarded in games of chance, provided that prizes may be identified on raffle tickets. [Source: Sec. 105-12]

****

60--*39.* Weird Laws -- Rhode Island

01. It is against the law to slit the nose, ear, or lip of any person. [Source: Sec. 1-29-1]

02. No wire shall be strung across a highway less than fourteen (14) feet above the surface of the highway. [Source: Sec. 11-22-15]

****

60--40. Weird Laws -- South Carolina

01. It is unlawful for a minor under the age of eighteen to play a pinball machine. [Source: Sec. 63-19-2430]

02. The sale or offer to sell the following items on **Sunday** is prohibited: Clothing and clothing accessories (except those which qualify as swimwear, novelties, souvenirs, hosiery, or undergarments); housewares, china, glassware, and kitchenware; home, business and office furnishings, and appliances; tools, paints, hardware, building supplies, and lumber; jewelry, silverware, watches, clocks, luggage, musical instruments, recorders, recordings, radios, television sets, phonographs, record players or so-called hi-fi or stereo sets, or equipment; sporting goods (except when sold on-premises where sporting events and recreational facilities are permitted); a yard or piece goods; automobiles, trucks, and trailers.

****

60--*41.* Weird Laws -- South Dakota

01. Movies that show police officers being treated in an offensive manner or being struck, beaten, etc. are prohibited.

****

60--*42.* Weird Laws -- Tennessee

01. It is against the law for any person to throw any stone, snowball, bottle at any tree.

02. The words animal or dumb animal is held to include every living creature.

****

60--43. Weird Laws -- Texas

01. A person cannot be excluded from holding office on account of his religious sentiments, provided he acknowledges the existence of a Supreme Being.

02. *City- Galveston:* It is against the law for any person in an aircraft shall throw out, drop or deposit within the city any litter, handbill, or any other object. [Source: Sec. 20-9]

03. *City- Galveston:* it is against the law to operate a bicycle at a speed greater than is reasonable and prudent under the conditions than existing. [Source: Sec. 9-4]

****

60--44. Weird Laws -- Utah

01. Causing a catastrophe is a felony of the second degree if the person causes it knowingly and a class A misdemeanor if caused recklessly. [Source: Sec. 76-6-105]

****

60--45. Weird Laws -- Vermont

01. *City- Barre:* It is mandatory for all residents to bathe every Saturday night.

****

60--46. Weird Laws -- Virginia

01. To hunt or kill any wild bird or wild animal, including any nuisance species, with a gun, firearm, or other weapons on Sunday, which is hereby declared a rest day for all species of wild bird and wild animal life, except raccoons, which may be hunted until 2:00 a.m. on Sunday mornings.

02. City- Frederick: You need a special license to sell watches, tableware, or other household items.

****

60--47. Weird Laws -- Washington

01. *City- Hoquiam:* It is against the law to tip the waitress/waiter more than 15% of the total price of the bill.

02. *City- Wilbur:* You may not ride an ugly horse.

****

60--48. <u>Weird</u> <u>Laws</u> -- <u>West</u> <u>Virginia</u>

01. It is against the law for any person to have in his possession or to display any red or black flag.

02. If any person arrived at the age of discretion profanely curse or swear or get drunk in public, he shall be fined by a justice **one dollar for each offense**.

03. Roadkill may be taken home for supper.

04. If somebody steals another man's horse, the owner has the legal right to hang the accused from the nearest tree.

****

60--49. Weird Laws -- Wisconsin

01. *City- Brookfield:* It is against the law to make or cause the telephone of another repeatedly or continuously to ring at the called number. [Source: Sec. 9.08.070]

02. *City-Hudson:* It is mandatory to use screens in your dwelling unit from May 1 to October 1 for protection against mosquitoes, flies, and other insects.

****

60--50. Weird Laws -- Wyoming

01. Individuals, firms, or corporations engaged in the buying or selling of junk metals, rubber, rags or paper, are prohibited from purchasing any articles from any person appearing to be intoxicated. [Source: Sec. 33-18-105]

****

If you discover life in outer space, including the moon, that may be hazardous to public health, you are required to immediately report it to the Secretary-General of the United Nations, as well as to the international scientific community.

****

<u>Weird</u> <u>Laws</u> – <u>A</u> <u>Jocular</u> <u>Saying</u>

"Everything which is not forbidden is allowed". [In England]

This transforms in some countries as the following:

"Everything which is not allowed is forbidden". [In Germany]

"Everything is allowed even if it is forbidden". [In France]

"Everything is forbidden, even that which is expressly allowed". [In Russia]

"Everything that is not forbidden is compulsory" [In North Korea]

****

About the Author

Manik Joshi was born on January 26, 1979, at Ranikhet, a picturesque town in the Kumaon region of the Indian state of Uttarakhand. He is a permanent resident of the Sheeshmahal area of Kathgodam located in the city of Haldwani in the Kumaon region of Uttarakhand in India. He completed his schooling in four different schools. He is a science graduate in the ZBC – zoology, botany, and chemistry – subjects. He is also an MBA with a specialization in marketing. Additionally, he holds diplomas in "computer applications", "multimedia and web-designing", and "computer hardware and networking". During his schooldays, he wanted to enter the field of medical science; however, after graduation, he shifted his focus to the field of management. After obtaining his MBA, he enrolled in a computer education center; he became so fascinated with working on the computer that he decided to develop his career in this field. Over the following years, he worked at some computer-related full-time jobs. Following that, he became interested in Internet Marketing, particularly in domaining (business of buying and selling domain names), web design (creating websites), and various other online jobs. However, later he shifted his focus solely to self-publishing. Manik is a nature-lover. He has always been fascinated by overcast skies. He is passionate about traveling and enjoys solo-travel most of the time rather than traveling in groups. He is actually quite a loner who prefers to do his own thing. He likes to listen to music, particularly when he is working on the computer. Reading and writing are definitely his favorite pastimes, but he has no interest in sports. Manik has always dreamed of a prosperous life and prefers to live a life of luxury. He has a keen interest in politics because he believes it is politics that decides everything else. He feels a sense of gratification sharing his experiences and knowledge with the outside world. However, he is an introvert by nature and thus gives prominence to only a few people in his personal life. He is not a spiritual man, yet he actively seeks knowledge about the metaphysical world; he is particularly interested in learning about life beyond death. In addition to writing academic/informational text and fictional content, he also maintains a personal diary. He has always had a desire to stand out from the crowd. He does not believe in treading the beaten path and avoids copying someone else's path to success. Two things he always refrains from are smoking and drinking; he is a teetotaler and very health-conscious. He usually wakes up before the sun rises. He starts his morning with meditation and exercise. Fitness is an integral and indispensable part of his life. He gets energized by solving complex problems. He loves himself the way he is and he loves the way he looks. He doesn't believe in following fashion trends. He dresses according to what suits him & what he is comfortable in. He believes in taking calculated risks. His philosophy is to expect the best but prepare for the worst. According to him, you can't succeed if you are unwilling to fail. For Manik, life is about learning from mistakes and figuring out how to move forward.

Amazon Author Page of Manik Joshi:
https://www.amazon.com/author/manikjoshi
Website: http://www.manikjoshi.com
Email: manik85joshi@gmail.com

Printed in Great Britain
by Amazon

10219438R00058